The Tears of Arakan

Between Me and My Ancestral Dwelling Place

The Poetry of
Pan Thar

Pan Thar

**

This book is dedicated to my dearest Rohingya people who face ongoing ethnic cleansing and genocide by the Myanmar (Burmese) security forces. It is written for those who are displaced from their homeland and to those who continue to hope for better and brighter futures.

**

*

Acknowledgements

*

I am truly and deeply grateful to Mikey Rose who helped me to publish my complete poetry works and made this dream come true.

Not to forget all my colleagues and sincere brothers and sisters that influenced me at my current poetry book.

Last but not the least, my all goes to my parents who made me the person I needed to be to crate and share this book.

*

PREFACE

*

The Tears of Arakan plead the world to express the struggle of Rohingya, to know Rohingya communities represent in the world, and to listen the voices of Rohingya people who have experienced the worst human right abuses. The Rohingya of Arakan have spent 2017-present under conditions of imprisonment; some are serving life sentences while others have been sentenced to death, some are dead, and others have escaped to Coxs Bazar. The return to Arakan is the truth of this book.

It's true that our society has been buried by the Myanmar (Burmese) government who pledge allegiance to evil politics. Unfaithful servants dine at the table of greed and selfishness and our homeland has become a stranger to its inhabitants. Nonetheless, I believe that all is not yet lost; for we still have the power to instil our discipline and correct those wrongs. Firstly, let's teach our Myanmar (Burmese) government to know the difference between knowledge, skills, and attitude. We must teach them moral ethics, hard work, good thinking, and selflessness and teach them to break from the path of the executives, workaholics, and entrepreneurs. We must widen their horizons on all different aspects of life.

Why can't we tell the Myanmar government that they need no validations to become successful and echo that half education is more dangerous than no education. We will teach them good policies for building a healthy nation, whilst correcting their wrongs and showing the need for a moral philosophy to uphold the norms and culture of our societies. What if we teach them how to become leaders and not rulers, with supportive laws and customs, rather than arrogance and false realities. In the meantime, they try to express themselves by building their missions and inspiring their harmful visions, yet we still have the power to turn water into honey.

A poet is a person who writes poems. A poem is a substitution, for better or for worse, for a lived feeling or event. It's a bunch of words that captures a moment in time or a feeling in unexpected ways. It's "a painting in words," or "a medium for self-expression," or "a song that rhymes and displays beauty."

In other words, a poem is an arrangement of words written or spoke; traditionally a rhythmical composition, sometimes rhymed, expressing experiences, ideas, or emotions in a style more concentrated, imaginative, and powerful than that of ordinary speech or prose; some poems are in meter, some in free verse.

Alhamdulillah, now we have nearly two hundred young and diverse poets in the Rohingya refugee camps. Living in the world's largest refugee camp in Cox's Bazar, Bangladesh, under unbearable circumstances, they try to express their pains, feelings, hardships, experiences, ideas, and emotions in their poetry.

Pan Thar is one among them, but he is also a student, humanitarian (health) worker, a teacher, and a photographer. Here he compiles some of his poems in English.

I hope and pray everybody will enjoy reading his words in this book.

Pan Thar

(Rohingya Poet & Humanitarian)

 Aman Ullah

(Rohingya freelance writer and researcher)

*

FORWARD

*

I am one of the over eight hundred thousand Rohingya people who crossed the border nearly four years ago. Before I witnessed this crime and injustice, I never believed that a man or a group of people could sit together and conspire to rob, blackmail, kidnap, murder or commit other acts of felony against fellow human beings. But now I know.

I have heard hundreds of my Rohingya's stories, but I see that many do not know how to explain their struggle to the world just because of education. Most of the characters referred to in this work, through fictitious names, are serving from 14 to 55 years imprisonment; some are serving life sentences while others have been sentenced to death and some are dead.

My words are an adieu to my country where I was born and lived from my very first day. I am surviving to share my Rohingya's stories and in hope for a safer place. Still, my whole life has become so dark that I struggle to see a future.

I'm a Rohingya Youth Student, Humanitarian Worker, Budding Writer (Poet) and Photographer, born on the 28th of February 1999 to Rohingya parents in Maungdaw Township, Northern Rakhine State (which is popularly known as Arakan State), Myanmar. Northern Rakhine State is where most of the Rohingya people live, but in this place my Rohingya community face ongoing violence, discrimination, and civil war. My beloved parents always encouraged me to learn more and more about this gloomy world. When I was a young baby boy, my mother tried to protect me from the world as it is really like today.

As I grew older, I have been confronted by a world in which every human right is denied to my Rohingya people and I have learnt how we, the Rohingya, are persecuted and discriminated against socially, politically, economically and by way of our religion. I managed to complete part of my education in a government-run school just because of the love and support of my dad, who has always been my hero. In 2017, I studied for matriculation in Maungdaw High School, but I was unable to take examinations because the civil war broke out on 25th August 2017. Sadly, due to differences of beliefs among war-mongering people, I wasn't given the same opportunities as the Buddhists in my homeplace.

The partition government of Myanmar in 2017, forced my Rohingya people to leave our ancestor's home when the communal riots were broken out in Maungdaw and elsewhere. My life is evidence that the security force clearance operation was systematic ethnic cleansing, and that many, if not all, the claimed attacks from Rohingya, were fabrications as a pretext for the military assault.

I took the brave decision to leave my country when my Rohingya people escaped to Bangladesh. It was not an easy journey and the cost of the boat fee from Myanmar to Bangladesh was 200,000 MMK in cash. The compartment of the boat was flooding, fully packed with my Rohingya passengers, who were also seeking survival in Bangladesh. On the way, I also lost contact with my siblings. The next day, when I reached Bangladesh, I had only a hundred Taka (BD) note left with me, which I had managed to conceal under my sock.

Travelling by boat, I distracted myself by contemplating my reflection in the water. First to the coast of the Naf-River where I spent a first night away from my country. I saw hundreds of thousands of my Rohingya people, who had become hopeless and dreamless, also crossing the border to Sha Por Dip of Teknaf, Cox's Bazaar, Bangladesh to save their lives.

I managed to wake up and drift; I felt pleased that, whilst on the boat, I could open my eyes and succumb to oblivion. I stepped out from the boat and walked towards a black door. Carefully, I slid my feet across the muddy ground. After a few hours, I was on the road again, long before sunrise. My destination was not a place to feel sleep turn a nightmare into a safer place. Still, I began hoping that I could be a Refugee among my fellow Rohingya, because I believe that blood is thicker than water. I knew I could be living among fellow Rohingya Refugees who are not my strangers.

Then and now, I feel fed up with people judging me when they don't even know about me. Questions circle in my mind as I push through the muddy alleys and low-hanging war crimes. I turned my face upward to investigate the blue sky. Suddenly, I'm overwhelmed by a feeling that I'm now like a seed buried deep in the dark earth.

I had arrived at a prison of my own pain. This did not surprise me as it had been told to me many times since I left my home.

My beloved Rohingya people from Myanmar were still pouring in when I reached Bangladesh. The local Bengali Muslims were very sympathetic to their uprooted fellow Muslims; the Islamic spirit of brotherhood inspired the Bengali Muslims to come forward with food, utensils, clothes, and other supports for my beloved Rohingya people.

Before leaving, my beloved parents, who are still in Myanmar, warned me to behave myself and not show off in front of them, but they could not keep me quiet. My mother seemed to think that she was defending her son. Bring my share so that I may pay for my plate. Things may turn hot, and each run their own way. As you said, I also thought that a great place was life without suspicion. You may burst in here for a few months.

I traced out Akter Hossain in a refugee camp located at Nayapara Registered Refugee of Teknaf in Bangladesh. He had made a refugee card to collect his daily meals from the gruel kitchen. For a few days I shared meals with him, until the supervisor of the camp asked me to go to Camp in Charge (CIC) to be registered as a refugee. We were registered as Forcibly Displaced Myanmar Nation's Persona (FDMNP) as this was all that was available for my fellow Rohingyas who had emigrated with me to Bangladesh. So, I didn't register as a Refugee and without a refugee card it was not possible to get admission freely in any school. My study was blocked down again there and I can't go back to Myanmar because of security reasons.

I remained for six months, getting to know several barmaids and sex workers in the Refugee camp as a Forcibly Displaced Myanmar Nation's Persona (FDMNP). During this time, I had changed greatly. For over 7 months, I had not visited home, nor had I got any reports from or about my people there. I did not even know the fate of my brother who, by then, had done his school certificate in class 7 to go from my village's school to Maungdaw High School. All that time, I was in Bangladesh.

Now, I was surviving in the tent of a Refugee camp and working as a Community Health Worker (CHW) to full-fill my old dream at FOOD FOR THE HUNGRY & MEDICAL TEAMS INTERNATIONAL(FH-MTI). As a CHW, I work very hard and struggle to save our Rohingya community from various kinds of health care. I have been able to help by getting training from FH-MTI. I'm really proud that I have an opportunity to join as a humanitarian worker/CHW in the organisation. They only give me a small amount of money at the end of each month, but this was not the problem. The problem was that my fellow Rohingya were in prison. The problem was that I did not know why I had earned this money, and for whom, if my siblings were not together. I had lost them on my journey and when I asked where they could have been taken resident to rescue their lives, I could not find all the answers.

After every failure, I say to myself, "if I get everything, maybe it was not in luck. So, I didn't get it. What a meaningless life! The intense pain of someone's leaving is hiding on a side of the chest and tell which happens for good. Why do I have to get pain for that good every time, I'm not done by myself! Whenever I understand, life is very random... I understand myself with my eyes, one day I will spend everything right... one day everything will be fine!!"

It's true that our society has been ruined by the Myanmar (Burmese) government who "pledge allegiance to evil politics, unfaithful servants dine at the table of greed and selfishness" and our homeland has become a stranger to its inhabitants, but I believe that all is not yet lost; for we still have the power to instil our discipline and correct those wrongs.

Enough is enough; enough, I say, "Every day and night I cry and go beyond myself and my painful story. I, myself was gone to kill for death. What kind of fucking life is this."?

Now, I'm going to start a new noble work, but I only have a vague idea of what I want to explore in my crisis. This idea has become clearer while writing as images emerge, characters, materials, and a plot evolve. I am pleased because something is better than nothing. I am writing these ideas so that they can be crafted into a compelling book, The Tears Of Arakan. When my book is complete, I really believe that you will understand my story of struggle and survival. I am motivated by this opportunity for creativity and introspection. Writing these words has made me something different, made me understand something I didn't know before.

While I was studying in Myanmar, I had a dream to be a doctor; to cure my Rohingya people, who are struggling to get better health care. This dream was to no avail. The partition government of Myanmar in 2017 forced my Rohingya people to leave their ancestors' home when the communal riots broke out in Maungdaw and elsewhere. I was treated unfairly. I was not given equal rights because of the Myanmar (Burmese) government. This forced me to change my dream and I now wish to become a poet; a poet who writes about the struggles and dreams of my Rohingya community who have emigrated to Bangladesh.

To achieve this dream, I became familiar with the different poetry platforms. The Art Garden Rohingya is the one I like best. It's a popular Rohingya poetry website for the Rohingya community, that also encourages me to be a good, remarkable Rohingya poet. I'm lucky enough to be a poet in my community in my young age. I owe this to Saya New Ali (Nur Kamal), who is one of my favourite Rohingya authors and tutors.

Between 21st February 2018 and 26th May 2021, nearly 250 of my poems and nearly 500 of my treasure of quotes have been published through different platforms. My poems are featured in the anthologies including ROHINGYA DREAMS, MY PEN SHALL TAKE ME TO THE STARS and NAMASTE INK. Arman Faisal Imran Khan (Aye Myint), Aye Myint, Ro Zaw Win, Mohammed Imran @Pan Thar.

The Tears of Arakan

Contents:

I.   Preface by Aman Ullah
II.   Forward by Pan Thar
III.   Rohingyas are not illegal immigrants by Aman Ullah
IV.   Aid Worker's Voices, Elon University
V.   I am a Rohingya
1. Adoror Bap Ma/ My Beloved Parents
2. I am a Lucky Enough...
3. I Seek Peace.
4. I Beg for Justice
5. That's Me, A Peacekeeper
6. The Rain
7. Black Trouble
8. COVID-19
9. The Stranger
10. Rape of Impunity
11. Independence Day of Myanmar
12. I am a Rohingya
13. Gallery One
VI.   I am a Survivor
1. I'm a Genocide Survivor
2. The Mayyu Mountain
3. "The Star"
4. Never Ending my Stress
5. My Heart Barks for Justice
6. World Refugee Day
7. Word
8. The Tarpaulin Shelter
9. Phoney Crony
10. Does Life Mean Breathing Only?
11. Hope for Future
12. Voice of a Survivor, Rohingya
13. Gallery Two
VII.   I Write for our Freedom

1. What Unity Can Change
2. I am a Feminist
3. Freedom in Education
4. Distress
5. Speak up for Refugee
6. Life is Precious
7. The Strength of Power By Heart
8. A Free Speech Defender
9. My Beloved Arakan
10. I am a Human Being
11. Gallery Three

VIII. Two Hands of a Rohingya Warrior – Mikey Rose

*

Rohingyas Are Not Illegal Immigrants - Aman Ullah.

*

Rohingyas are descended from local indigenous tribes who lived in Arakan since the dawn of history. The Arabs arrived in Arakan in the late 7th century AD, settled there and intermingled, intermixed, and intermarried with the local people and converted several local populations including local Buddhists. The appearance of the Arabs in Arakan in the 7th century was more of a cultural phenomenon than an ethnic one. The Persians, Turks, Pathens and other Muslim migrants who came into Arakan in the course of time also merged with the local populace. These various migrations and local conversions led to the formation of a common grouping classified as "Rohingya"; a term derived from Rohang, the ancient name of Arakan.

The Rohingya tradition is over 1300 years old. It is a personal tradition of culture, history and civilization expressed through shrines, cemeteries, sanctuaries, social and cultural institutions found scattered even today in every part of the land. By preserving a heritage as distinct from Buddhist spaces, they formed their own society with a consolidated population in Arakan well before the Burmese invasion of Arakan in 1784.

Jacques Leider, in his article, 'Between Revolt and Normality: Arakan after Burmese Conquest' mentions that "we admit of a total population of Arakan of circa 250,000 in the time of (the Burmese) conquest, the country steadily lost up to 50% of its population. English observers estimated the Arakanese population at about 100,000 at the time of the British conquest."

Eaton, in his book 'The Rise of Islam and the Bengal Frontier' argues that "Perhaps up to three-quarters of Danra-waddy's population by the 1770s may have been Muslim." But According to Professor Michael Charney of University of London, "Although there is very little evidence of a rural Muslim community in Arakan prior to the 1570s, they clearly made up a substantial proportion of the population in the 1770s, prior to Burman rule."

According to a British government document on the cultures and inhabitants of Arakan by the Secret and Political Department, Fort William dated 26th April 1826, "The population of Arracan and its dependencies Ramree, Cheduba & Sandaway does not at present exceed 100,00 souls, may be classed as -- Mughs six tenths, - Mussalman three tenths, - Burmese one tenth, Total 100,000 Souls." As to Mr. Paton, Sub Commissioner of Arakan, who submitted this report from Akyab, "The extent of the Population has been tolerably well ascertained, proved a census taken by Mr. Robertson, and myself, and may be considered as approximating very nearly to the truth.

This means that among the 100,000 souls there is a split of: Mughs 60,000, Muslims 30,000 and Burmese 10,000. According to Professor Michael Charney, "When we adjust for the absence of large numbers of Muslims in Rama-waddy, Mekha-waddy, and Dwara-waddy, however, the proportion of Muslims in the Danra-waddy zone's population was probably much higher." So, in the date of conquest of Arakan by the British, there remained thirty-thousand Muslims and these thirty thousand Muslims were living there from before, now their descendants and successors have increased leaps and bounds.

According to the censuses of both 1921 and 1931, it is clearly sustained that, 'There was a Muslim community in Arakan, particularly in Akyab District, who prefer to call themselves Arakan-Mahomadens and are quite distinct from the Chittgonians and Bengali immigrants to Arakan.' 'According to a Baxter report of 1940, paragraph 7, "This Arakanese Muslim community settled so long in Akyab District had for all intents and purposes to be regarded as an indigenous race."

Indigenous peoples were the descendants of those peoples that inhabited a territory prior to colonization or formation of the present state. Hence, these Muslims of Arakan, who identify themselves as Rohingya, are for all intents and purposes to be regarded as an indigenous race and are also a racial group who had settled in Arakan/Union of Burma as their permanent home from a period anterior to 1823 A. D. (1185 B.E.).

Being one of the indigenous races and bona fide citizens of Burma, the Rohingyas were enfranchised in all the national and local elections of Burma except 2015 and 2020 elections: - during the later colonial period (1935-1948), during the democratic period (1948-1962), during the BSPP regime (1962-1988), 1990 multi-party election held by SLORC and 2010 General Election held by SPDC. Their representatives were in the Legislative Assembly, in the Constituent Assembly and in the Parliament. As members of the new Parliament, their representatives took the oath of allegiance to the Union of Burma on the 4thJanuary 1948. Their representatives were appointed as cabinet ministers and parliamentary secretaries.

Legislative Assembly Election of 1936

The first and only election held under the Government of Burma Act 1935 took place in November 1936. Before 1937, Burma was a province of British Indian Empire. In 1937 Burma was separated from India under the British Administration. A new constitution came into effect. Under its provisions the people of Burma were given a bigger role to play in the running of their country.

Under the 1935 Act there were 132 seats in the House of Representatives, 91 of the seats were general non-communal seats and the remaining 41 were reserved for communal and special interest groups of which 12 were reserved for Karen (of Ministerial Burma), 8 for Indians, 2 for Anglo-Burmans, and 3 for Europeans.

However, according to Martin Smith, 'there was no separate representation for the Mons of Lower Burma; the question of seats of the Southern Chin, the Arakanese Muslims including Kamans and Myedus, the Zerbadis from the mixed Burma Muslims union. The single exception has been North Arakan, where Muslims from distinct majority constituency in several districts along the Bangladesh border.' {Martin Smith, Burma: Insurgency and the Politics of Ethnicity 1999}

Thus, the Rohingya Muslims of Akyab district North constituency, a non-communal rural constituency, were recognize as children of the soil and in the first time taken as eligible to vote or to stand for election on the ground of their being one of the indigenous communities of Burma. Mr. Ghani Markin returned on the votes of those Rohingyas as a Member of Legislative Assembly.

Constituent Assembly election of 1947

The second election was held under the Aung San-Atlee Agreement that was signed on 27 January 1947. According to that agreement, which said, 'in order to decide on the future of Burma a Constituent Assembly shall be elected within four months instead of Legislature under the Act of 1935. For this purpose, the electoral machinery of 1935 Act will be used. Election will take place in April 1947 for the general non-communal, the Karen and the Anglo-Burman constituencies as constituted under the Act of 1935, and each constituency two member shall be returned. Any Burma nationals defined in the 'Annex A' of the Agreement registered in a general constituency other than one of those mentioned above shall be placed on the register of a general non-communal constituency."

According to 'Annex A' of the Agreement, "A Burma National is defined for the purpose of eligibility to vote and to stand as a candidate at the forth coming election as British subject or the subject of an Indian State who was born in Burma and reside there for a total period not less than eight years in the ten years immediately preceding either 1st January 1942 or 1st January 1947".

Immediately before the last election, the Muslims of Akyab district North constituency were recognized as children of the soil and first taken as eligible to vote or to stand for election on the ground of their being one of the indigenous races of Burma, but when the Aung San - Atlee   Agreement was out, the government misunderstood the position and it was notified that unless they declared themselves as Burma nationals, they would not be eligible to vote or to stand for election to the constituent Assembly.

The Muslims of those constituencies protested vehemently against this decision on the ground of their being one of the indigenous races of Burma. The government withheld the first decision and allowed the Muslims to vote or stand for elections held in March 1947. Mr. Sultan Ahmed and Mr. Abdul Gaffar returned on the votes of this Muslims as members of the constituent Assembly. They continued in their office, representing the Akyab district North constituency till Burmese independence and took the oath of allegiance to the Union of Burma on the 4th of January 1948 as members of the new parliament of the Union of Burma.

Parliamentary Elections during 1948-1962

From the holding of the constituent Assembly until 1962 when the military took over, three general elections were held for both Chambers of the Parliament in 1951, 1956 and 1960, respectively. The Rohingyas had enjoyed the right to vote and the right to be elected in all the elections. In 1951, Mr. Sultan Ahmed, Daw Aye Nyunt (a) Zohora Begam, Mr. Abul Bashar and U Poe Khine (a) Nasir Uddin were elected as members of the Chamber of Deputies and Mr. Abdul Gaffer was elected as a member of the Chamber of Nationalities. In 1956, Mr. Sultan Ahmed, Mr. Abul Khair, Mr. Abul Bahsar and Mr. Ezahar Mian were elected as the members of the Chamber of Deputies and Mr. Abdul Gaffer remained as a member of the Chamber of Nationalities. A by-election was held for the Buthidaung North Constituency in 1957 as the election of Mr. Ezahar Main was challenged, and the verdict was given against him. Mr. Sultan Mahmood was elected, and he was inducted in the cabinet of U Nu as a Minister of Health. In 1960, Mr. Rashid Ahmed, Mr. Abul Khair, Mr. Abul Bahsar and Mr. Sultan Mahmood were elected as members of the Chamber of Deputies while Mr. Abdus Suban was elected as a member of the Chamber of Nationalities.

General Election during 1962- 1988 in BSPP Regime

During the Burma Socialist Programme Party (BSPP) regime, four general elections for the People's assembly and People's Council at different levels were held in 1974, 1978, 1982 and 1986, respectively. These elections had been held with regards to the 1974 Constitution.

Under the 1974 Constitution and 1973 Election Law, "citizens born of parents both of whom are Union nationals and citizens born of parents both of whom are Union citizens, have the right to be elected people's representatives to the People's Assembly or People's Council at different levels. Persons who are not citizens of the Union of Burma have no right to vote."

According to the 1974 Constitution, "citizens are those who are born of the parents who are nationals of the Socialist Republic of Union of the Burma and who are vested with citizenship according to existing laws on the date of this constitution comes into force."

Former Minister for Mines Dr. Nyi Nyi and Deputy Minister for Foreign Affairs Minister U Win Ko had to resign from the position of the members of cabinet and People's Assembly, as they could not fulfil the requirement of the said law.

The Rohingyas had enjoyed the right to vote and the right to be elected as people's representatives to the Organ of State power at different levels. No Rohingya who had either been elected or who had applied for the nomination had been challenged or barred from participation or asked to resign after being elected.

Multi-Party Election of 1990

SLORC held multi-party general election in May 1990. The Rohingya were not only allowed to vote but also, in their exercise of franchise, elected four Rohingya members of Parliament. U Chit Lwin (a) Ebrahim, Mr. Fazal Ahmed, U Kyaw Min (a) Shomshul Anwarul Haque, and U Tin Maung (a) Nur Ahmed have been elected as members of the Parliament.

The 1990 election was held in accordance with the 1982 Burmese Citizenship Law. Under the 1989 election law "all citizens, associate citizens and naturalized citizens are permitted to vote, but only the citizens are allowed to stand for election. No foreign residents were allowed to vote." Thus, the participation of Rohingya people in the national elections must be upheld as a measure of recognition for the Rohingyas as full citizens even under 1982 Citizenship Law.

In fact, the Rohingyas were not only permitted to vote but also to form their own political parties during the May 1990 election. Two parties were formed the Students and Youth League for Mayu Development and the National Democratic and Human Rights (NDPHR). The NDPHR won all four seats in Maung Daw and Buthidaung constituencies, and in each constituency votes for the two parties counted for 80 per cent of the total votes cast. Moreover, the turnout in both constituencies equaled the national average, at 70 per cent of eligible voters. The NDPHR also fielded candidates in four other constituencies; Kyuk Taw-1, Minbya-1, Mrauk U -2 and Sittwe -2, and they gained an average of 17 per cent of the votes while the Government- backed National Unity Party got only 13 per cent.

Although the name of Rohingya was not permitted to use in the party title, the NDPHR was allowed to produce a booklet in Burmese called 'Arakan and the Rohingya people: a short History' on August 31, 1991.

General Election held by SPDC in 2010

A general election was held in Burma (Myanmar) on 7 November 2010, in accordance with the new constitution. This constitution was approved in a referendum held in May 2008, which was held during Cyclone Nargis.

Since 2008, Brig-Gen Phone Swe, Deputy Minister of Home Affairs, was assigned to assess the conditions in Northern Arakan and to organize the peoples residing there for the constitutional referendum. Brig-Gen Phone Swe managed overwhelming support from Rohingyas 2008 constitutional referendum to the satisfaction of the junta. They want the same support and cooperation from Rohingyas at the coming 2010 election with joining Union Solidarity and Development Association (USDA) a political affiliate of SPDC.

A total of 37 political parties contested in this election, which included two Rohingya political parties - - National Democratic Party for Development (NDPD) and National Democratic and Peace Party (NDPP). Some independent Rohingya candidates also contested in the election.

Out of the 33 Rohingya contesting in the polls, 21 contested with NDPD ticket, 6 with USDP ticket, 3 with NDPP ticket and 3 independent candidates. U Htay Win (a) Zahidur Rahman with USDP ticket was elected for the Nationalities Parliament. U Aung Zaw Win (a) Zakir Ahmed and U Shwe Maung (a) Abdul Razak both with USDP tickets were elected for the People's Parliament. U Aung Myo Myint (a) Jahan Gir with USDP ticket, U Aung Myint (a) Zahiddullah and U Bashir Ahmed both with NDPD tickets were elected for the State Parliament. The Rohingyas of North Arakan had overwhelmingly gone to vote with average turnover of more than 90%.

The citizenship issue was a settled issue and the Muslims of Arakan who identify themselves as Rohingya are citizens by birth. As they, their parents and their grandparents were born and bred in Burma and most of them were indigenous, under the sub clauses (i), (ii) and (iii) of Article 11, of 1947 Constitution of Union of Burma.

These are fundamental rights of a citizen and the 1947 constitution provided safeguard for fundamental rights. Under this constitution, the people of Burma irrespective of 'birth, religion, sex or race' equally enjoyed all the citizenship rights including right to express, right to assemble, right to associations and unions, settle in any part of the Union, to acquire property and to follow any occupation, trade, business, or profession. Rohingyas are not illegal immigrants in Myanmar, rather they have been produced as illegal by the world.

Pan Thar

*

Aid Worker's Voices – Tom Arcaro, Elon University

*

October 27, 2020

"I communicate and work with many Rohingya poets and poetesses who are writing poetry for various platforms. Our writing makes us not only feel glad but also to be proud of our activism for our community. Our pens are our guns. Our words are our bullets. Our ink is our activism."

-Pan Thar, Rohingya poet

Bringing two worlds together: Par Thar, Rohingya poet

In the past 18 months I have been in contact with many young Rohingya men and women now living in the world's largest refugee camp in Cox's Bazar, Bangladesh. Most are victims of genocidal persecution from the Myanmar government and military, fleeing along with over 700,000 other Rohingya to Bangladesh in August of 2017.

I have written many posts about what I have called 'refugee humanitarians' and have kept up with the lives of most via social media. I continue learning about the human rights struggles of the Rohingya and am following the genocide case against the Myanmar government now being examined by the International Court of Justice.

Refugee camp life is hard, and there are many pressures to succumb to the negative forces swirling about the narrow pathways between the bamboo and plastic sheeting houses. Many Rohingya women and men demonstrate great resolve and strength, daily fighting those forces. For every act of violence in the camps there are hundreds of actions, both big and small, which never make the news. I have been privileged to meet (virtually) many kind, compassionate, and brave Rohingya souls.

Meet Pan Thar, one shining light among many.

Last week I noticed a Facebook post highlighting a poem recently published in the Art Garden of the Rohingya by a young man named Pan Thar. I commented on the poem, mentioning that I would talk about it to my university sociology classes. The poem addressed self-identity and the need to be in control of one's destiny, both topics we have examined.

Via Facebook Messenger, we talked. Below is part of the discussions we've had.

Here is what he wrote describing himself:

"I, Pan Thar am a Rohingya youth student, Humanitarian Aid-Worker, Photographer and budding writer (poet) of the present generation and writing is my passion. Faced by racism I was born to Rohingya parents in Maungdaw, Northern Rakhine State (also popularly known as Arakan State), Myanmar where most of the Rohingya people live. My Rohingya community was facing violence, discrimination, and civil war for decades. I want to be one of the most educated people in the world to create peace and harmony for the entire world."

I learned from Pan that he has written over 250 poems since he started putting pen to paper in 2018. Many of his poems have been published in online sites such as The Art Garden of the Rohingya, Litlight, Speaking Heart, Arthut, and Namaste Ink. Though he has published under various pseudonyms, he now "strongly admits it is me, Pan Thar."

Pan Thar is his newest pen name, based on his home village in Myanmar.

I asked, 'How do you find the time and energy to write your poems?'

"When I get free from my work, I love to spend my time by composing poems and stories to express and let the world know, how we, Rohingya are surviving in the world largest refugee camp of Cox's Bazar, Bangladesh and how much we were tortured by the Burmese government. I'm a genocide survivor and non-citizen of in this darkness world. So, I do not get such an opportunity to hold computer and smart phone freely, but I write my poems and stories by pen into paper."

How important to you is it that your words are read and heard? What does not mean to you to be published?

"Being a persecuted people, it is very important to me to read and hear my voice get out all over the world. If not so publish my words to the world, they would not know how much I was tortured in my birthplace and [experiencing] suffering in camp yet."

Have you worked for any INGO humanitarian organizations like IRC, MSF or DRC? If so, can you tell me about that work?

"I work as a volunteer, as a Community Health Worker (CHW) under the UN Organization called Food for the Hungry and also Medical Teams International (FH & MTI) by day and I teach History at the Free School For Rohingya Community (FSRC) by night. Both are my professions to help my community to improve and show their talents for the entire world. I choose this both work to help my people who didn't get enough health care and proper education. When I work in the field to improve my community for their health care, I seek to change their negative mind for a better understanding what people must need to change and to improve the entire world day by day. When I'm in the class to teach our historical book, my younger generation don't know how we need to note, and we forget what we faced genocidal operation in our birthplace and for what, but I teach them again and again to remember what we need to change our world."

He goes on,

"The project of Joint Rohingya Respond Program (JRRP) was organized by Food for the Hungry and Medical Teams International (FH & MTI) to help the most vulnerable Rohingya people.

One my ambitions was to become a doctor to cure my people but [I am] unable because my brutal government don't give us [the opportunity] to study. However, today, I can help other Rohingya through the organization for their health. In this pandemic situation, we want to add more information, there are still misconceptions and misunderstandings about mentally in our society.

What are your thoughts about your repatriation? Can it happen?

"We are so grateful to the Bangladesh government for saving hundreds of thousands of souls from the danger, but we all want to go back home to our birthplace, Myanmar. But we must work to get our human rights. A Bengali poet says, 'Born anywhere is a citizen of everywhere. This universe is ours.' So, repatriation must be possible for me and my people who are in Cox's Bazar Refugee Camp if we get all our human rights. If not so, I'm far away from it."

How close are you to the other poets in the camps? Do you work with them?

"I communicate and work with many Rohingya poets and poetesses who are writing poetry for different platforms. Our writing makes us not only feel happy, but also to be proud of our activism for our community. Our pens are our guns. Our words are our bullets. Our inks are our activism.

How are you dealing with the corona virus? Are the big NGO organizations doing a good job?

"Here in the refugee camp, all the shelters are near to each other, and it is crowded here. So, it is hard for us to maintain distance from each other, but we are doing our best. And because of the lock down, it is also hard for us to go outside to buy things. All the NGOs are working their best to protect us from corona by providing masks and soaps, doing sessions on social distance and how to be safe. They also built isolation treatment center for the suspected corona virus patients.

What family do you have? How do they feel about your poetry activities?

"I was born to a poor family who was always eager to be educated. My beloved parents are Mr. Mohammed Younus (High School Teacher) and Mrs. Hafsa Bibi (Private Teacher) who are encouraging me to learn more and more about this darkness world. They always feel proud with me for being a poet and are encouraging me to fight for our rights through poetry."

Trading classroom visits

I read the Pan's poem "I Am Rohingya" to my class on Thursday and then Friday morning (here in US) Pan invited me to meet his class via FaceTime. I joined his class briefly and said hello to his students. He and I talked about education and teaching. Pan and are similar in that we are both teachers and learners.

A call to witness

I have been trusted by many Rohingya to hear and then sometimes share parts of their story. That said, I am a witness to an ongoing genocide. My incomplete and very humble response to what I witness is to constantly seek to learn more so that when I do have the opportunity to amplify voices I do so with fidelity to the truth and with all the grace I can muster.

I am reminded of the words of James Dawes. In **That the World May Know** he notes, "...giving voice can also be a matter of taking voice." He goes on, "This contradiction between our impulse to heed trauma's cry for representation and our instinct to protect it from representation –from invasive staring, simplification, dissection – is a split at the heart of human rights advocacy." Indeed.

Full article at: Aid Worker Voices / Bringing two worlds together (elon.edu)

https://blogs.elon.edu/aidworkervoices/?p=1690

Part I:

I am a Rohingya

A Note on Rohingyalish:

All the ethnic groups on the face of this earth have their own tongue. We Rohingya have also our own Mother's Tongue called Rohingya language that we use to communicate each other in our community in Arakan state and in any part of Myanmar where we Rohingya live.

As I'm a Rohingya poet, I write poems in my own language that is Rohingya language. In this book here a poem in my Rohingya language could be found to let the world know that we Rohingya have our own language that in Arakan state Rohingya communicate in this language.

Adoror Bap Ma (Rohingyalish Translation)

Añr Adoror Bap Ma...!

Oñnorah sára hono Shantír

Moza buzí nófarír

Uçèr oñnorar yadgari

aró zorèr sukor fani.

O Añr Adoror Bap Ma...!

Añttún nai sukot fani

Oñnorarlah haintè haintè

Hono waktót fórai no fari

Monót uçèr oñnorar yadgari

O Añr Adoror Bap Ma.....!

Añttún uçrè wañarar yadgeri

Gura halor túnáró bèshí

Zodi Eid ór ainda aiyle

Aró bèshi monot forè.

O Añr Adoror Bap Ma...!

Fotti èkkán khúshir haalot

Monot uçèr oñnorar yadgari

Awshánti lói aró zorè sukor fani

Oh Añr Adoror Bap Ma...!

Añttún nai sukot fani

Oñnorar lah haintè haintè

O Añr Adoror Bap Ma...!

Nizorgá nizè haçi fèaláir

Hainte hainte oñnoraré hoi

Sena burèr sukor fani loi.

O Añr Adoror Bap Ma...!

Ar no gojjo sinta

No Oiyo awshánti

Zètodin añi aseí

O Añr Adoror Bap Ma...!

Añttún uçèr woñarar yadgari

Oñnora sara hono Shantir

Moza buzí nófa

The Tears of Arakan

My Beloved Parents (English Translation)

O' my dearest parent... !

Without you, I feel no peace

Drop tears drop and

You are remembered

O' my Beloved Parents... !

I have no tears left

by crying and crying for you.

I can't forget anytime

and you are remembered

O' my dearest parents... !

I am remembering you the most

even before growing up.

When Eid (Festival) comes

I remember you the most.

O' my Beloved Parents...!

In every happiness time,

You are remembered the most

and tears drop my eyes by sadness.

The Tears of Arakan

O' my dearest Parents...!

I am losing myself

My chest is covering with tears

by crying and crying for you

but where are you

O' my beloved Parents...!

till I alive.

Never feel worried

and don't be sad

O' my dearest Parents...!

You are remembered

without you, I feel no peace

O' my beloved Parents...!

no tears drops in my eyes

by crying and crying for you.

Pan Thar

I am a Lucky Enough...

Being born to Rohingya parents
I'm a lucky enough person
who was rejected all the dignity
being the same human like you all.

Being born to Rohingya parents
I'm a lucky enough person
who was hacked all his property
being the same human like you all.

Being born to Rohingya parents
I'm a lucky enough person
who never feel peace once
being the lack of education.

Being a human like you all
I want to bring peace and humanity
but I never feel it once
just for the lack of education.

The Tears of Arakan

I, myself want to be an educated person

to create change by pen

But never got a chance of it

what kind of human am I?

Thinking, thinking and thinking too much

why I was born in this world of darkness

To reject all my opportunities,

to reject all my dignity,

to reject all my peace and freedom?

Being human like you all,

How am I a lucky enough person?

Pan Thar

I Seek Peace.

I am a Rohingya

I am like a prisoner

Living my life in melancholy

Drowning in my tears

And no one to rescue the dying me

I am as an orphan

Whose happiness has been fleeced off

I desire peace,

Even as little as a drop of water,

Would brighten my dark days,

And paint my despair with hopes.

I dream of a peaceful Nation

Void of discrimination

Where wars and

Rumours of wars

Holds no water.

I dream of a Nation,

Abounding in love and peace.

I Beg for Justice

Since decades in my nation,

The terrorism of the terrorists

Enlarging to all the nation

I was killed by hurling to fire

Where my dream was killed

But still remaining the same

I scream loudly to hear my voice

The year of twenty seventeen,

The launcher shoots to my home

The village burned down to ash

where I can't survive by life of fear

That harm to my blameless heart till the time

where surviving with full of fear in jungle

I'm still screaming to the world

And I beg the world for justice

The year of twenty seventeen,

I was given my blood for the nation

Which is totally espy of the nation

For the world to step for justice

Pan Thar

I scream loudly to hear the world

None give attention to my voice

What is my fault of being still helpless?

The struggle is facing for decades

The country has broken promise to pain

and resist to all part of the nation till

I beg the world to stand against the injustice

where thousands of souls have been taken

billions of people made homeless and hopeless

I scream to the world for justice.

That's Me, A Peacekeeper

I need peace to brighten my future,

Without discrimination elsewhere.

I have no one to rescue me,

My tears are the water of the ocean.

Being Rohingya is like a prisoner.

Without pillar with sincere love,

Me, a people facing discrimination

In my beloved nation by the government.

Spending my life in the forest like criminal,

Why don't cease promoting conflicts,

Being a Rohingya?

When I had lived in Myanmar,

My mind always floats to a dream

To celebrate the world void of war.

Being a Rohingya,

I shoot myself, teared of sorrows.

Yet, I have no mother like orphan

To understand my struggle what I face.

A droplet of peace what I'm seeking

Give me peace, no more discrimination

It's beautiful me as a civilian in my nation.

#Photo - Medical Teams International - (23.02.2020)

The Rain

I wonder when rain drops fall

from where they're coming

and how they're made

how a wonderful rain you are!

A rain of arrows

by the cloudy sky

makes me feel joyful

how a wonderful rain you are!

The garden is made green

by scattering thy rain drops

where I feel my being cheerfully plays

how a wonderful rain you are!

The forest wakes so noisy

and the green sprays shook

no tears and delightful

how wonderful rain you are!

My life is growing somewhere

by getting trouble pain

where I can't see you, rain.

How a horrible life I spend.

Black Trouble

I was born in depression,

For love my tireless sunshine.

I was born in a noisy morning,

love came as a soothing silent night

Being born in this prison-earth,

that tells only saddening verses.

born to a minority Muslim people of Arakan

Does it mean to face the genocide?

Show me a bird that sings about sorrow

Tell it to console this broken prisoner of the earth.

Let it dirge about a living dead

sadness, a friend of date since birth.

Nothing to say about my childhood,

I lost my teenage at its birth,

to a profound spread of grief,

With so much anxiety nailed to my fingertip.

Pan Thar

Tell this not to my predators,

let my pain become their humour.

Let this perfect picture of sorrow

be painted by a poet without laughter,

for grief has shamed happiness.

I'm being overwhelmed by worries

Each of my woes is likened to a woodland

that continuously loses shape to these decorated black flames,

that camouflages dazzling beauty

In reality a catalogue of pain.

The ribs are named after those assemblies

I've arranged a safety-match chest.

Published in The Art Garden Rohingya (16.12.2019)

COVID-19

COVID-19 is a pandemic disease

It's spreading all over the world

People are isolated and quarantined.

The countries can't save a life

Some people say it's a pandemic

But I think it's god-give wrath (aba viyaram)

The countries are in lockdown

For the fear of COVID-19 infection.

We can't stay safe in broken tents.

It came originally from China

Spreading all over the world

People are in million dead

The USA and Italy are on top

Of number of cases and deaths

No treatment, no antidote for it

Just awareness sessions are going on.

It's a powerful mind, Anti-Corona

That would be prevented from its affection.

Pan Thar

The Stranger

It was not easy

It was not an opportunity

to enrol unknown heartbeats

It was happening for Newton's law

Is it not for me?

It wasn't easy to just calm down

It doesn't matter just in love

The pain is full in the chest

I couldn't get it yet

Let's take it into fun

It is a prayer of mine

If not really with you,

I don't want to smile without you.

Rape of Impunity

Poet's Note: This poem is dedicated to a Rohingya rape survivor from Gu Dar Pyin massacre carried out by Myanmar Tatmadaw against Rohingya villagers in August 2017.

I'm a young Rohingya girl

I was gang-raped

my parents were massacred

by the Burmese military

during the crackdown in August of 2017.

Three years has been passed,

I am still crying not for my pain

but just to hear the world that:

violence, discrimination and injustice

are ended over me and my people.

My mother and I were raped together

My father was killed

My brothers were shot to dead

And I'm a lonely survivor from

too much horror of injustice.

My village was burnt down

Pan Thar

Hundred of my villagers were massacred
It's too horrible for me
to survive a single life
in my village where I grow up.

Red and black into my nation
where trees cannot change the colour
but the colour was changed into red
with the blood of my body
and it's become black and dark.

In that very year,
my blood gets a big hand
to illustrate my painful process
which will be a strong enough
for the world to prove of genocide.

My life falls into anxiety
unendurable for my civilians
It makes me a fighter
against the injustice and violence
of my bloody Tatmadaw.

The Tears of Arakan

It is too hard to forget

and not so easy to admit

and still keep on struggling

but never give up,

I still cry and beg for justice.

Pan Thar

Independence Day of Myanmar

Since Burma got independence,

73 years have passed

many poems, stories, and songs

have been written differently

many rose to the stage year by year

nothing has change for the Rohingya yet.

Birds can live on their nest

without the fear of injustice

and with their dignity of freedom

We, Rohingya can't live in our home

with our rightful dignity and peace.

What is the independence

of Burma and for whom?

Birds can fly in the distant blue sky

From here to there.

Since I was born, I'm a prisoner

and was rejected every human rights

I was discriminated and neglected

bound in a tight chain of subjugation

The Tears of Arakan

the language of the desires

My mouth was silent of fears

Am I just deserving of Genocide?

Rohingya love their nation and respect it's flag

where their forefather give them birth

who roar in the same mantra for independence

Painting the highway with fresh blood in the chest

They brought freedom in silence

Students, teachers, farmers, workers, fishermen, weavers,

Burma, Rakhine, Rohingya and other ethic people

all are the same as brotherhood,

this soil of ours is soaked in the blood of all

who is your own and a different race.

I keep talking about to whom

who do compare with and inferior of dignity

who is the herald of independence

and who do it's lesson.

The nation knows that in 1948

Myanmar gained independence

now, we're running back year by year

where they forget the principles of justice

and now, violence, hatred, politics, and religion discrimination

I am throwing everything confused today

Even living in an independent country

Do I get any taste of it today?

Freedom of expression,

The proverb of humanity is being plunder!

what kind of nation, Myanmar with terrorists Tatmadaw.

I am a Rohingya

Poet's Note: This poem is based on my Rohingya life in Myanmar.

I'm a Rohingya

Born to Rohingya parents

In Myanmar, Arakan State

Where violence, discrimination

and the civil war taking people's lives

In Myanmar, by face I'm named Bangali

In Bangladesh, by culture I'm named Burmese

In the mouth of UN by whom I survive,

My name is 'refugee'.

I'm confused for what they named me

unacceptable for a true inherent person

Who is full of evidence in hand

That proves and names me;

That is a Rohingya,

A descendant of my ancestors

The dignity that my body

and my desire waiting to bear

Once from all by a name

That is a Rohingya,

A descendant of my ancestors

In talking my heart doesn't listen to it,

A fake name that makes me imitation

In shape and the way of whole life

Get suffered within my community

Just watching to let you all know that

From where I am descended

And by which name I'm named

That is a Rohingya,

A descendant of my ancestors

Beyond me, it is mixed in the wilderness

Since I was born, I've been a prisoner

Just like my parents and grandparents

I'm in a hundred of galaxies,

My free residence is nowhere over the planet.

Raising my infinite power of miserable arms,

The Tears of Arakan

My life crashed down facing second genocide?

Give me your light where I can secure my life.

Being a minority in Myanmar

Does it mean to face another genocide?

When my tears touch the cracking ground,

In despair, my heart drowned

As the clear blue sky darkened

My life is full of agonies and fierce storms

Hopelessly weary away from a distance.

Touching the untouchable art

I sigh reaching deeply my floppy heart;

The illusion of classical dance that hurts

To all my friends,we will never be apart

For my writings to you, I sincerely dedicate

As I express my humble gratitude

When time comes I will be in solitude

Let my writings reside in your mind

To complete the evolution of my creation.

This is the real 'me',

A Rohingya myself

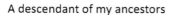

Pan Thar

A descendant of my ancestors

Published in The Art Garden Rohingya (21.10.2020)

Pan Thar

Part II:

I am Surviving

Pan Thar

I'm a Genocide Survivor

From the end I stand.

Building my own history.

A way of pillar made of sadness

And windows of regret.

Social sunlight peeks upon me,

through the sunshine on canvas.

But I see only a visible coloured image;

Recovery a mirage, sailing through the waters

I think maybe we'll walk again.

Flooding my mind, an unknown dust.

The smell of a useless tune

suddenly turns around my path,

sleepy heart loses its way to the ears.

Yet, the finger calls Arakan

To light years.

History blowing

as black and white dream.

The Tears of Arakan

Sleeping in self-made dreams,

waking up and returning home,

only in self-made

Stories, poems, and songs

All dreams staying as dreams.

Even though some dreams die day to day.

For Long, long ago,

we forgot the smell of soil.

Now my dreams as a sinking horse,

running into the geographic heart.

Sneaking and taking little peek from reality

Now I understand

By touching the fur of cats,

how much more I will eat the stench of sheep

In the atmosphere!

That's me in my genocide survival history!

Finally educated, my salutation

Is to know what we really want?

The death of relative has happened,

sometimes I again and again wish for death,

Because the end will be the history of living.

The Mayyu Mountain

On the lap of Arakan, I was subsisting.

Where Mayyu Mountain is situated.

Which split twice Maungdaw into Buthidaung.

Today, I'm recognized by it's rubric

But have to live in camp way of it.

When it appears in my dream at night,

I surmise, my head is taken in its lap

But find nothing at morning

Except the pillow drenched in my tears.

Do you ever hear about it?

It's like a curtain that inculcates empathy

Of both sides' residents

Like siblings from one family.

It's compared to neither bank nor jewellery

Because the necessities of life are freely fulfilled.

Hi Mayyu Mount!

Let me breath your breeze again.

I'm your kid Rohingya from your land Arakan.

Pan Thar

Remember! My soul never gets satisfaction in the grave

Unless it's behest is fulfilled

That's only to be buried of my dead body

In your lap, Mayyu!

"The Star"

Poet's Note: The poet used "You" to indicate "the Star".

The sky is so cloudy

and you are hidden

To light my wonderful ground.

But you always do twinkling.

I'm a human with body but no dignity

Like you twinkle but no light

To accost where my humanity

But I'm drowning in the ocean for my right.

O' why do you go abroad?

Missing you so much for light

If you went to my lord,

Give it back to us, we want.

Who can come by singing the song!

That it looks like the sugar for a long life.

You take as much as you want

Although there is no more as I want.

It's humanity and peace in my life.

Never Ending My Stress

I'm inside the car

Without a driver

to fulfil my greatest wish

up to my final destination.

I'm in a random thought

Where, I know not

but never lose hope

and still on the trip

I find a motorman

who hides the truth of reality

my stress is arising

And never ending is my stress.

My Heart Barks for Justice

Deep inside, I'm innocent

No one should judge me

Before they understand my pain.

No one understands my situation,

My explanations on deaf ears.

Just because I'm a Rohingya.

They look down upon me.

All forced situation, confined

What about the man who perishes on me?

My heart barks out of pain,

They were there, I bark for justice

They just laughed at me,

Because I'm persecuted and a refugee.

Now I'm in the arms of judgemental society,

Why don't they accuse and isolate them,

Just because they are influential.

And me, for being a Muslim minority

I'm still barking for justice,

Just to live again in my Arakan

Pan Thar

In peace and freedom

Published in The Art Garden Rohingya (22.12.2019)

World Refugee Day

Is the world gloomy for a refugee

or a people of minority

But Why, I afraid of losing my authority's home.

Naver again!

What a gloomy world for a refugee!

No more, I want to be.

Not for me, not for my people

But for my darkness world

who are flooding into gloomy days.

Pan Thar

Word

Dear world,

The midday is so clear,

but my heart is still in fear.

The cosmos is so blue,

but my heart can't find a word

to say where my mind and death

Dear world,

Your words are so sweet

It's may be humanity

It's may be reality

My mind can't find a word

to say where it is for me

Dear world,

I'm a flooding bird

to find the word of my right

I'm hoping that what I feel

even though I am a Refugee

where is my humanity.

The Tarpaulin Shelter

My tarpaulin shelter

Under the open sky

Without water

And shadow of the three.

In the summer season,

No safe water and air

To stay with a healthy life

Too hot that can't we feel

And affect me to the pain

Inside my tarpaulin shelter.

In the rainy season,

The tent is ruined by the strong air

And it floods with water

No shelter to stay with a healthy life.

Phoney Crony

How lovely this love is, lovely and loving

It happened for the first time,

it happens only once

it won't happen again in my life

the one who has stolen my heart

appears at night as a dream

My love in my life

How crazy this love is, crazy and crazing

It went crazy for the first time,

It makes me only once

it won't make me again in my life

the one who has underrated my sense

appears in my sight as hope

The cure in my life

How thirsty this love is, thirsty and thirsting

It got me thirsty for the first time,

It gets me only once

it won't happen again in my life

The one who has reversed my joy

appears ahead of my life as chance

My light in darkness

Published in The Art Garden Rohingya (29.11.19)

Pan Thar

Does Life Mean Breathing Only?

Being a human like you all,
I was rejected all my dignity.
Breathing on this world
like a lifetime prisoner.
Does life mean breathing only?

I'm a human like you all
Still denying every single human rights
If no one offer me about education,
Why then am I here, in this world?
Does life mean breathing only?

Being a hungry for education,
My government called me a criminal.
If I have no education in my life,
how can I manage my life?
Does life mean breathing only?

Being a minority Rohingya people,
neither an opportunity to learn
nor to travel anywhere.

The Tears of Arakan

Why then am I here, in this world?

Does life mean breathing only?

No... no... no...

I'm a human like you all

Give me an opportunity

to learn education

So, I may manage my life

Is this world or hell?

What a fucking life I spent!

Now, I'm seeking justice

to have opportunities like you all.

Being the same human,

I'm deserving to get back the right.

I have responsibility to change my world.

Life means not only breathing,

Offer me my education.

If I'm educated, I will bring peace and harmony

for the entire world.

Pan Thar

Hope for Future

The world has busted the time again

Stories are quoting on the newspapers again

When I sleep, I can't see my peace

Flying without my own ale in air

My tears are dropping into the world

To repose trust into my Lord

who can save my life come a long way

to spend to the right ways.

My heart isn't dead yet,

but the body again and again

Me, the bird isn't flying to my aim

How can I save my life again.

The infant is crying when he is born,

the mother is cringing in labour of pain

Father is depriving too much

I, myself can't tolerate the pain

To bright the epoch is my endeavour

with my education what and where I can

To rack the morale, rule, and education

on my forehead for my future.

Published in The Art Garden Rohingya (23.09.2020)

Pan Thar

Voice of a Survivor, Rohingya

Me, A criminal for the world

Yes, but do you ever realize me

for what I'm a criminal?

Being a minority or uneducated people?

Yes, I'm a criminal of my country

but do you ever offer me

to be an educated people

to bring humanity for the entire nation?

I have a hunger of education

to bring peace and harmony

but none offer me it once

how I will be a literate people?

Yes, I did crime for you

but it isn't discriminated to you

Being born to illiterate people

is my crime or what?

The Tears of Arakan

Who think about me?
If you, why you don't offer me,
to be a criminal for the world?
Where are novel owners
who talk about education of entire world?

I, myself seeking for education
none hear my sorrowful voice?
Becoming a criminal is my mistake or
No offering for my education is a mistake?

You are a real criminal for me
just because no offer me for education
to create changing my community.
You, my government is a real criminal!

The Tears of Arakan

Part III:

I Write for Our Freedom

What Unity Can Change

Unity can build peace

For there are more questions

Even after death, it will ask more

If we don't try to act on time

We will surely fail in peace

Unity can change the society

For there are more questions

Even after death, it will ask more

If we don't raise our voices together,

Our society will leave us in peace

Unity can educate society

For there are more questions

Even after education, it will ask more,

If we don't educate ourselves together,

Our society will wallow in divided arrogance

Unity can fight the society,

For there are more questions,

Even after we rise, it will ask for more

Pan Thar

If we don't fight our arms together,

Our society will hallucinate in its strongest ability.

I Am a Feminist

Poet's Note: This poem is dedicated to all the women of our community on the occasion of WORLD WOMEN'S DAY.

Many of my Rohingya people

Who recently crossed the board of Myanmar

To get back their basic human right.

Many of my Rohingya femininity were there

Who are facing different kind of struggle.

The most wonderful creation of almighty

On this planet with a soft and kind heart,

They are even my mother, daughter, sister,

Their treat with dignity and respect.

Being females, they can't study in our community

We woke up around past for the future

Take their path and prepared for their literacy

They are the left-over concoction of study

Let women empowerment and get established

Their future in our society with gender equality,

Don't make the inroads, thinking about their future

Pan Thar

Freedom in Education

Poet's Note: This poem was written in a meeting of Development Campaign with Department for International Development (UK aid - From the British people) sharing our challenges of education who are hungry of education.

To this nation I call mine

Your freedom I love like wine

Give me education, that I may become all you desire

Give me Quality education to make me

A soldier, guarding your territory like mother hen

Protects her chicks from their predator

A physician, administering cure to every emotional ailment

All I desire is freedom

Let education be for all

Without segregation between the rich and poor,

For the healing of the dumb and illiterate minds

Education is the mother of civilization

It reflects in our character like blood runs through our veins

It submerge our ignorance in the well of knowledge

The Tears of Arakan

Give us quality education that comes with freedom, for without it,

Our cultural growth will be retarded

Our development will be limited

Give me quality education

For all I desire is a free nation

Photo by - Muhammad Zubair

Pan Thar

Distress

Arakan is my ancestral dwelling

But my existence has known no freedom,

For the world itself cannot

A wave of sorrow

that sleeps in my heart.

In this perilous time,

Fear and despair ravage my heart.

And pain blurs my future

For my eyes have seen,

The youth fall prey to corruption

broken dreams littered in streets,

Children whose body tell sad stories.

I've sought for salvation

And I have found none

My heart hungers for the truth,

For it, my freedom is assured.

Published in The Art Garden Rohingya (25.06.2020)

Speak up for Refugee

From time to time

woke up with Refugee

they have their own stories

to talk and tell the world

Speak up for Refugee

Even have eyes, we can't see

Even have mouth, we can't talk

Even have ears, we can't hear

Refugees have their lifematter

Speak up for Refugee

Hand for solidarity

can change the world

We still have power

to speak up loadly

for the world Refugee.

Life Is Precious

This life, God has made

Is precious to enjoy

The earth been precious

Is full of life heightened sense

Let the poor seek ultimate

Peace with their grace

Let the weak aspire

To rise and not despise

Their weaker souls to stone

In quarry heat in the sun

Life is precious

And needs every glimpse

Of time in rich for the price

Of making them to shine

So no power should shake

The foundation of the poor

They're weak and sad

Under the leaders' hearts

The Tears of Arakan

Refuge is their common place

To have their bread of the day

I will feel the pity

Like a chaotic street

To see women cry

In the anguish of their sons

Life is already precious

And the world has reason

With every human being

So why imprison the poor?

In solid cages of no space

Why enjoy their toil?

As leaders of no joy

I tell you, please the poor

And give them pace to love

Their freedom of exalted lives

This I cry thou free

For those who are not

Pan Thar

So let us free the souls

In prison of no fault

Published in The Art Garden Rohingya (25.10.19)

The Strength of Power by Heart

The day and night,

increasing prolonged scare

in the face of injustice

to be free with a peaceful life.

I fight to bring liberty

in my patriotic nation

which will testify erratic death

for peace to incapacity life

The fast word of my life

seeking the real justice

to my brilliant county

where is the solidarity.

I am an eyesore of humanity

who wants to bring their promises

but charity has failed the civilian

who works raising a pen for calm

The extreme pain of cruelty

by witnessing a coup of the nation

Even if in the face of unmerit,

still fighting for democracy.

A Free Speech Defender

Poet's Note : The poem is dedicated to the global leader who are peace lovers and freedom fighters for the people of this darkness world.

He who works for the helpless people

to get back their basic right

what people must have

is a freedom moment of their life.

He who works for the voiceless people

to raise their voice

and to hear their voice in the world

what they want to talk.

He who works for the glare

to bring humanity for the global people

to change this gloomy world

with the beauty of human.

He who is a freedom fighter

want to train humanity

to ignore injustice

for the entire community

Pan Thar

He who is a peace keeper

to build harmony

without a limitations of life

for the global community.

My Beloved Arakan

The first time when I saw you fully

A great blossom of garden

Shining like the stars in the sky

Birds are flying

to take branch in the shade of the tree

Singing birdsong with their sweet voices

So pleasure to see and listen to it

Every time I look at your face

It illuminates like the sun of the day

Every time I look at your green garden

It glamours like the moon at the night

How I wish you can experience my dream

I can't stop confessing how you make me happy

Now, I look on you for what I saw

No trees longer where I saw a green garden

You seem like the bloodbath ground

Are you made looking-bad to see?

I can't stop my tears about you.

Pan Thar

Oh my adorable life-span garden!

When you can regain the green garden

I'm in the prison to leave from you

So dangerous to live here

Like an anaemic animal in the zoo

I can't stop my crying about suffering.

Fish can't live without water.

Human can't live without air.

In my refugee life, I pass my time

Through squalid crowd they whisper,

I can't live without my motherland

Just because you're in my blood

I can't stop my heart where I breathe for my life.

Published in The Art Garden Rohingya (16.11.19)

I am a Human Being

Poet's Note: I wrote this poem by reading EXODUS, authored by Mayyu Ali. In EXODUS, all poems are very touching and remind me the genocide on me and knowing the value of a Human Being.

Better living in nature

Than to live among human beings

I know how to love people

There is nothing called love.

I knew to be generous to my people

Not to be generous on arbor of man.

Those times who are in medieval

He killed all my bonafide people.

How much I faced with the torture of rip

So why, I never forget

You say, people are for people

If so, who are they around me?

I learn to be a human being to my people

Nowadays, I love much to my own way

On the streets of the road

Pan Thar

Only the procession of death
Only deprivation to my city.

To me, human being is cruel,
Human existence, without identity
You say, people are for people
If so, who are they around me?

All pains are received through deprivation
Death torments in closed door
Finally, I am a human like you
And innocent like you
You believe it, I am still a human
I want to live by being a human being.

Published in The Art Garden Rohingya (16.01.2020)

A Rohingya Warrior - Mikey Rose

This collection of poetry is more than an ensemble of words. These are thoughts, feelings, and experiences. These are the expressions of a human being. A human being who has lived a multitude of intersecting and parallel lives; lives which amount to beauty, community, brutality, love, horror, and survival. Lives that are in constant movement, whilst resting in states of expression. The author of these songs is a young Rohingya warrior, who goes by the penname Pan Thar. His art is political, fierce, peaceful, and just. His voice expresses the real and coherent interests of not only himself, but also his Rohingya communities. Despite the hard work of oppressive and dominant power structures, Pan Thar speaks...Rohingya people speak. Read his poems and listen.

When I first spoke to Pan Thar, I asked him where he was living. His response turned the question to highlight the flaw in my engagement. He was not living, he was surviving...surviving in the world's largest refugee camp in Cox's Bazar Bangladesh. Living requires free and malleable space unavailable to so many Rohingya people. Surviving is resistance; it is holding truth to the little space you do have whilst everything around you tries to break it. In Taiaiake Alfred's words: "survival is ending and swaying but not breaking, adapting and accommodating without compromising what is core to one's being."[1]

As an infant, Pan Thar dreamed of serving his community in Maungdaw as a doctor. This inspirational drive to support the welfare and health of his people is core to his being. As a person of Rohingya ethnicity, this dream was forcibly denied by the discriminatory and violent order of the Myanmar (Burmese) State. Under these conditions, Pan Thar, like all Rohingyas, was not only unable to access the necessary education or qualifications, but also faced immediate danger in the form of economic, health and military violence. Forced from his home, he sought safety in neighbouring Bangladesh. Whilst he has been able to join millions of his fellow Rohingya people at the refugee camp in Cox's Bazar, he has not found safety.

The refugee camp is built and organised as temporary, yet reality structures this space as void of hope and futurities. It is a space of waiting, turning bodies into

---

[1] Alfred, T (2009) Wasase pg.29

subjects of dependency, whilst punishing for the same thing. States around the world refuse to provide necessary support; they refuse to listen to the interests of Rohingya people; actively denying the existence of such independent interests. Repatriation is discussed away from any consultation with Rohingya people and without any material or practical investment (which countries like the U.K. can so readily afford to offer).

Warriors such as Pan Thar disabuse this notion of Rohingya helplessness and absolute dependency. Pan Thar picks up his pen, which he metaphorically compares to a gun, and releases his pain, his experience, his interests through resistance: "My pen is my gun. My word is my bullet. My ink is my activism." Yet he is not alone. He is encouraged, inspired, by members of his community and shares this love of words with them. Before he started writing there were only four Rohingya poets that he was familiar with. Now there are hundreds.

The power of writing, particularly for Pan Thar, is in its mobility. Whilst Rohingyas are trapped from movement, living in limited and constantly diminishing space, words offer freedom; "they can go anywhere and everywhere." Through writing, Rohingya can present themselves to the world, offering liberation from outside representations. These words are not simply retorts fed in opposition to the Tatmadow, which commits atrocities on behalf of the Myanmar State, they are strategies of territorial expansion. For with every word written by Rohingya, Rohingya space expands.

Pan Thar's poems are not an end in themselves. As well providing space for personal expression, this poetry feeds into a wider struggle for Rohingya resurgence. Pan Thar fights not only with his pen, for with his other hand he looks to build the young members of his community through education. "Unable to study in Burma," "Rohingya people are very under-educated." Education is further limited in the camps, with spaces described by Pan Thar as "playing places" rather than "learning places." There is no curriculum offered to support Rohingya teachers and UNHCR programs are focused predominantly on basic early learning. The responsibility Pan Thar feels to share the education he has managed to gather is immense. Everyday he finds a quiet place in the camp, where he can provide some schooling to the younger generation of Rohingyas. He has no curriculum, but he can connect with and pass on a shared wisdom – teaching how to live together. This act is a struggle, with little to no funding he lacks access to basic teaching materials. Yet he, like many people in his community, prevails and continues to form and serve the interests of his communities. It is this process of future building, through the imaginings of a free Rohingya that expands Rohingya space, creating room for not just surviving but living.

Myanmar, or Northern Rakhine State (Arakan) more specifically, is central to any discussion of Rohingya spaces. This is the home that remains fixed whilst swaying through movements of power. The military coup this year has been devastating for Rohingyas, including Pan Thar; it is a moment that he compares to the arrival of a storm. Despite the NLD's unforgivable complicity in the persecution of Myanmar's minority ethic groups, it is with the Tatmadow that full culpability lies. Any potential return home is only narrowed by the prevalence of this coup. However, Pan Thar recalls a proverb: "when the storm comes, the ants unite and become untouchable." This moment, in many ways, is appearing as one of opportunity for solidarity and real change. Before January 2021, Burmese citizens rarely accepted the Rohingya name; instead, reproducing persecutory state propaganda. Now there are clear signs of this changing, including the National Unity Government's consideration of a Rohingya representative. These are minor wins, but they represent a real shift in popular perceptions. Burmese activists are building for solidarity with Rohingya people, showing active recognition of the vast military complex that has served to violently marginalise Rohingyas and enable an anti-democratic coup.

Pan Thar's voice is one of a million Rohingya voices that must be heard and met in resisting state, military, and all oppressive power. These poems are not just a collection of empty words, they are political statements, they are human experiences, they are expressions of survival and strategies of liberation.

Mikey Rose, PhD Candidate at University College Cork

Printed in Great Britain
by Amazon